IMPRESSIONIST LANDSCAPES

The Custom Officer's House at Varengeville, 1882, Monet.

IMPRESSIONIST LANDSCAPES

JUDE WELTON

STUDIO EDITIONS
LONDON

This edition published 1993 by
Studio Editions Ltd
Princess House, 50 Eastcastle Street
London, W1N 7AP, England

Designed by Michael R Carter
Printed and bound in Singapore

ISBN 1 85891 012 9

INTRODUCTION

Painting landscapes in the open air, direct from Nature, was central to the art of the Impressionists. With their portable easels, canvas, palettes and paints strapped to their backs, the Impressionist artists left behind the confines of their studios and strode out to work *en plein air* (in the open air). Often setting up a large umbrella to control the fall of light on the canvas as they worked, they strove to create direct, vivid impressions of the world as they saw it.

In their attempt to capture the fleeting effects of Nature – the ever-changing light conditions, the breezes rustling the trees, the movement of the rippling waters of the River Seine – the Impressionists adopted a new way of painting that was much more rapid and sketchy than the laborious, meticulous techniques of the traditional art against which they rebelled.

Their landscape paintings were generally smaller than those of the past, as canvases painted outside the studio had to be small enough to carry.

The Impressionists were not the first artists to paint landscapes out of doors: throughout the nineteenth century, artists had made rapid oil sketches in the open air. But these were mainly intended as studies, rather than as finished paintings. Most landscapes before those of the Impressionists were painted in the studio – some based on open-air studies, some composed according to an idealized concept of what a landscape ought to look like. A number of painters of the generation before the Impressionists had already rejected idealized images and created pictures which reflected their direct response to Nature. The Dutch artist Johann Barthold Jongkind, for example, was very influential on the young Claude Monet, one of the leading figures in the Impressionist group, encouraging him to paint out of doors. Jongkind himself completed his pictures in his studio, after open-air studies, but as the critic Jules Castagnary said, 'With him, everything lies in the *impression.*'

By the 1860s, when the future Impressionists were art students, open-air painting had become something of a craze in France. Popular countryside areas near Paris, recently made accessible to city dwellers by the newly

Flood at Port-Marly (detail), 1876, Sisley.
Note the strong colours of the watery reflections of the building and the sky.

invented trains, were dotted with amateur and professional artists at work, as well as with Sunday picnickers. Around this time, the novelists and diarists Edmond and Jules Goncourt wrote revealingly, 'Finally, we found a corner where no landscape painter was sitting at his easel, and there was no slice of melon left behind.'

The Forest of Fontainebleau, about an hour from the capital by train, was a favourite place for *plein-air* painting expeditions. It was here that the so-called Barbizon School of landscape painters had been based since the 1830s, at the rural village of Barbizon. The future Impressionists admired these artists greatly, but while the landscapes of the Barbizon painters reflected a 'return to Nature' and a rejection of the urban world, the Impressionists wanted to create landscapes that made some reference to modern life.

Rather than being timeless images of lonely trees and remote, wooded glades, Impressionist landscapes virtually always contain some sign of a modern human presence – a yacht, a distant house, a train, even a factory. Most of the time, the Impressionists painted the landscapes they knew best – those that lay close to home. Monet, for example, painted the meadows and the Seine at Argenteuil, and later in the countryside around Giverny;

Sisley devoted his career to painting the riverside villages outside Paris; Pissarro focused on more rural scenes in and around Pontoise.

The vogue for open-air landscape painting that occurred around the time of the birth of Impressionism was partly due to technological developments in the paint industry. Before the 1840s, oil paints were kept in pigs' bladders: when the bladders were pierced with a pin, the paint tended to dry up quickly on exposure to air. But with the invention of airtight tubes for oil paint, prolonged outdoor painting sessions became more practical.

Advances in paint technology also led to an extended range of pure, vibrant colours, which were favoured by the Impressionists. Painting in broken, rather than blended brush strokes, they used the colours they observed in the natural world, rather than those that objects were assumed to be. They were fascinated by the way colours changed according to their surroundings and by the way shadows appeared coloured in reality – not grey as they were conventionally shown in art. This concern with colour can be seen in the shimmering reflections in the river Seine, which appears so often in their art; in images of dazzling red poppies set in brilliant contrast against green meadows, or in the multi-coloured whites of snowy landscapes.

The Impressionists were always a loosely knit group, and in the 1880s, they broke up, with individuals going their separate ways even more than previously. But the practice of painting out of doors remained, and influenced artists who followed. The so-called Post Impressionists – as Seurat, van Gogh, Gauguin and Cézanne were labelled after a group exhibition of modern art in 1910 – found continuing inspiration in Impressionist landscapes, but they all wanted to move beyond a concern with atmospheric effects and surface appearance.

Like the Impressionists, Seurat used paint to recreate visual effects, but he pushed the idea so far into the realm of optical theory and science that his works negate the original spontaneous spirit of the Impressionist landscape. Cézanne's repeated pictures of Mont Sainte Victoire reveal his preoccupation with depicting the underlying structures and relationships of Nature. Like Cézanne, Gauguin worked closely with Pissarro in his early years, but later he moved away from his Pissarro-inspired landscapes towards paintings that evoke something of the mystery of life. In van Gogh's paintings one can see how the artist extends and exaggerates the bright colours and distinctive brush strokes of Impressionism to create extraordinary images of the external world that express his own, often tormented, inner landscape.

Cornfield with Cypresses (detail), 1889, van Gogh.
The artist has used broad brush strokes and brilliant colours to great expressive effect.

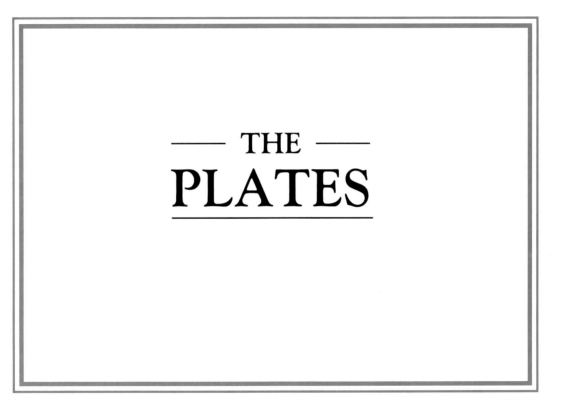

—— THE ——
PLATES

PLATE 1
Frédéric Bazille
Landscape at Chailly, 1865

Bazille had been an art student at Charles Gleyre's teaching studio in Paris when he and his fellow-students Monet, Renoir and Sisley made their first painting expeditions in the Forest of Fontainebleau in 1863. He painted this powerful landscape two years later, when he and Monet had returned to the forest, and were staying at the village of Chailly, two kilometres from Barbizon. The 24-year-old artist's choice of an isolated corner of a wood, and his relatively dark colours owe much to the work of the Barbizon painters who had been established in this area for three decades. But in painting his picture entirely out of doors, in his concern for capturing open-air effects, and in his broadly handled, unblended brushstrokes, Bazille looks forwards to Impressionist landscapes. He would undoubtedly have become known as one of the great Impressionist painters had he not been killed in the Franco-Prussian War in 1870.

PLATE 2
Johann Barthold Jongkind
Seascape, with Ponies on the Beach, 1866

Jongkind's finished paintings maintained the appearance of spontaneity and immediacy, even though they were actually composed in the studio after preliminary studies made out of doors. This vigorously painted, atmospheric 'marine' is typical of his work. Jongkind's concern with capturing the specific atmospheric conditions he observed, and his loosely applied, sketch-like brushwork make him an important forerunner of Impressionism. 'To him,' Monet said, 'I owe the final education of my eye.' Here, the Dutch artist vividly portrays a chill, breezy day on a rather unpicturesque stretch of Normandy beach, where village men lead a string of ponies along the shore, ready to transport the goods that are being rowed ashore from the clippers anchored in the bay.

PLATE 3
Berthe Morisot
The Harbour at Lorient, 1869

Painted during a summer visit to her sister Edma at Lorient, this little picture so impressed Morisot's mentor and future brother-in-law Edouard Manet, that the artist gave it to him as a present. Although an early work, it already reveals Morisot's characteristically subtle, pale-colour harmonies and her astonishingly free brushwork, particularly in the treatment of the stone parapet on which Edma sits. The figure of Edma herself, shaded by a parasol like so many women in Impressionist landscapes, is painted with daringly broad strokes of white, pale pink and pale violet. She gazes down into the sky-filled reflections on the pastel blue water. In the distance, counterbalancing this boldly worked, isolated foreground figure, are precisely rendered tall ships, delicately painted buildings and tiny promenading figures.

PLATE 4

Armand Guillaumin
Sunset at Ivry, 1873

Many of the artists who exhibited at the eight so-called Impressionist exhibitions held between 1874 and 1886 have never achieved the fame that was eventually granted to figures such as Monet, Renoir, Sisley and Pissarro. Guillaumin was one of these 'unknown Impressionists'. Like his close friend Pissarro, with whom he painted at Pontoise by day while digging ditches by night to earn a living, Guillaumin was inspired by industrial landcapes. But his approach to the subject differs from that of his friend. This is an essentially traditional, scenic view, in which distant factory chimneys form a dramatic silhouette against a blazing gold sunset, the intensity of which reflects Guillaumin's taste for strong, often gaudy colours. There is a powerful sense of dynamic tension created as the distant smoke clouds drift to the left, while the river sweeps forwards to the right, the brilliant sunset reflected in its dark waters.

PLATE 5
Claude Monet
Wild Poppies, 1873

One of the most famous images in Impressionist art, this charming painting shows Monet's young wife Camille and their six-year old son Jean walking through a field of poppies near their home at Argenteuil. It is a summer's day, and Camille is shown carrying her open parasol, as usual: its distinctive shape adds to the painting's decorative appeal. Brilliant red poppies have been dabbed on to the thinly painted green grass to form a triangle that cuts the picture in two. The figures appear to move quietly down the hillside, along the diagonal. Monet has included a smaller, more distant couple, also modelled by Camille and Jean, at the top of the hill to increase the sense of movement.

PLATE 6
Camille Pissarro
Hoarfrost, 1873

This tranquil scene shows a local worker carrying a bundle of faggots on his back, toiling up the hill on the old road to Ennery at Pontoise. A haystack peeps over the hill, indicating that the season is autumn or early winter, and Pissarro's title tells us that it is early morning, before the sun has melted the frost. When Pissarro painted his picture, the old road to Ennery had been replaced by a newer route, and had dwindled to a path. Indeed, it is difficult to discern the road at first: under the shimmering layer of frost, it almost merges with the furrowed autumn fields. The subject itself shows no trace of the modernity that features in many Impressionist landscapes. But Pissarro has used an artistic device that was strikingly 'modern' at the time: by including shadows cast by a row of poplar trees that stand outside the picture itself, he suggests the world that continues beyond the frame.

PLATE 7
Claude Monet
The Railway Bridge at Argenteuil, 1873–4

Its pink-grey steam set against pale clouds, the train from Paris puffs over the River Seine at Argenteuil. Monet had moved to this riverside suburb, about a twenty minute train ride from the capital, in 1871, and the eight years he lived there were the most prolific of his early career. He painted local river scenes many times, working on the Seine itself, either in the special floating studio he had had built or setting up his easel on the riverbank, as he has done here. Trains and railway bridges recur in his work during this period: potent symbols of modern life, they also represented the link between town and the suburban countryside which was a central feature of Impressionist art.

PLATE 8

Camille Pissarro

Landscape near Louveciennes, c.1875

The village of Louveciennes, some seventeen kilometres to the west of Paris, was one of the most important sites in the development of Impressionism. In the late 1860s, Pissarro, Sisley, Renoir and Monet all painted in the area, and many Impressionist landscapes depict local scenes. Although this painting is traditionally called *Landscape at Pontoise*, and dated 1875, the brushwork and the predominantly dark, brown-and-green colouring make it more likely that it was executed between 1870 and 1872, when the artist was based at Louveciennes. Pissarro had not then begun to use the lighter 'Impressionist' colours of his later works. The centrally placed path leads the eye into the picture, a familiar device in Pissarro's art, curving past the young girl and her goat towards the rather grand farmhouse beyond. At first sight, this appears to be an image of timeless country life, but closer inspection reveals that the foreground is a construction site, a sign of impending change amid the rural calm.

PLATE 9

Pierre Auguste Renoir
Path Climbing through the Long Grass, *c.*1875

Despite obvious links with Monet's *Wild Poppies*, this lovely, summer
landscape reveals the differences as well as the similarities between the
two friends' work. There is a delicacy and a fluid, feathery softness in
Renoir's technique that contrasts with Monet's bold application of more
solid areas of paint. Both artists have included two sets of figures walking
downhill and diagonally across the canvas, but Renoir's figures merge
more gently with the landscape, and take their part in the more subtle
pattern of colours that enlivens the composition. As in Monet's painting,
the artist has exploited the vivid contrast beween green and red, but in a
less aggressive way. Where Monet's poppies form a distinct red triangle in
the bottom left of the canvas, here the brilliant red of the woman's open
parasol is echoed in lighter touches of red dotted throughout the picture.

PLATE 10

Pierre Auguste Renoir
On the Banks of the Seine, Champrosay, 1876

Renoir's primary artistic interest was in portraits, and his landscapes usually exist as an enjoyable natural setting for his figures. But some canvases, such as this one, are celebrations of unpeopled country views. Despite the cloud-filled sky, the scene is imbued with a brilliant summer light, an effect which Renoir has created using pure, bright colours. Dividing the composition in three with the diagonal of the riverbank and the line of the horizon, he has varied his brushstrokes in each section. Bold strokes of green and gold create a powerful, swirling rhythm that sweeps up from the bottom of the long reeds or grasses, leading the eye into the middle distance. Rapidly applied horizontal dashes of blue and green are used for the river, while roughly scrubbed areas of blue-mauve, blue-green and pink describe the cloudy sky.

PLATE 11
Alfred Sisley
Flood at Port-Marly, 1876

Unlike his friends Monet and Renoir, Sisley never achieved commercial success. Yet, along with Monet's 'Wild Poppies', this, his masterpiece, is among the most celebrated of all Impressionist paintings. It is one of a number of pictures he made of the spectacular flood that took place in the spring of 1876, when the Seine burst its banks at Port-Marly. The flood waters have risen to cover the rue de Paris, where Sisley has positioned himself directly across the road from the wine merchant's shop. Despite the implicit drama and danger of the situation, with heavy clouds promising more rain, the muted tones and beautifully balanced composition give the picture an air of peace and calm. The left side is dominated by the solid structure of the building in the middle distance, its ochre walls reflected in the choppy, grey flood water; the central section opens out to lead the eye across the silvery-blue reflections to the horizon; to the right a slender telegraph pole and a row of half-submerged trees mark the foreground plane.

PLATE 12
Camille Pissarro
The Banks of the Oise, near Pontoise, Cloudy Weather, 1878

The landscapes that Pissarro painted in the 1870s often show the rural world of Pontoise being transformed by industrial activity. Unlike his friends Monet, Renoir and Caillebotte, Pissarro was always more interested in creating images of labour rather than of leisure. And in this quiet scene, he contrasts traditional and modern aspects of a working landscape in a way that suggests that the old is capable of absorbing the new. A local man in waistcoat and soft hat is carrying a bundle of faggots he has gathered for fuel. On the far bank, seen through a gap in the screen of autumn-bare trees that spreads across the picture, a man and his horses continue the rustic theme. But to their right is a factory, its tall, smoking chimney caught up in the tangled pattern of branches in the foreground.

PLATE 13

Paul Cézanne

The Bay of Marseilles seen from L'Estaque, c.1878–9

When he displayed his work at the first and third Impressionist exhibitions of 1874 and 1877, Cézanne gained little but critical abuse. He withdrew from Paris and spent more and more of his time working alone in his native Provence. Preoccupied with underlying structures rather than with the fleeting effects or shimmering surfaces of Impressionism, he said that he wanted to treat Nature 'in terms of the cylinder, the sphere and the cone'. This landscape, one of many versions of the same view, reduces the scene to its essential geometry. The panorama appears to be flattened against the canvas, with the densely coloured triangle of water wedged between the angular range of mountains in the distance, and the wooded slopes of the foreground. The simplified form of chimney stack in the foreground accentuates the sense of geometry in the composition.

PLATE 14
Camille Pissarro
Landscape at Chaponval, 1880

Dressed in her blue peasant's smock and bonnet, a young woman tends a grazing cow in the dappled shade of a summer meadow. The village of Chaponval, where this view was painted, lay between Pissarro's home at Pontoise, and Auvers where his younger friend Paul Cézanne had moved in 1872. The two men worked together closely, and though Cézanne always regarded himself as the older artist's pupil, their work shows a strong mutual influence. Cézanne's concern with simplification, geometry and interconnecting spatial relationships is echoed in this landscape. The angular shapes of the houses and their blue and red roofs form a geometric band across the centre of the canvas. Indeed, Pissarro has treated the entire landscape as a series of flat horizontal bands, unifying the picture surface with short, directional strokes of paint.

PLATE 15
Alfred Sisley
The Small Meadows in Spring: By, *c*.1880

In 1880, Sisley moved south of Paris to the village of Veneux-Nadon near Moret-sur-Loing, the area in which he was to remain for the rest of his life. This delightful scene is one of two almost identical compositions he made of a meadow path that ran from Veneaux to the nearby hamlet of By. (Today the path has become a paved road.) Wooded riverside paths became a favourite subject for Sisley, and here he has employed the traditional device of using the path to lead the eye into the picture. But the sense of movement into the landscape is halted by the girl who stands to the side of the path, her shadow cutting across its receding diagonal. It is a delicate, airy landscape, redolent of spring and although the trees remain almost leafless, their warm pink and gold colours suggest emerging foliage.

PLATE 16

Claude Monet

Lavacourt under Snow, *c.* 1878 – 1881

Monet was fascinated by all atmospheric effects – morning mists, dappled sunshine, the subdued atmosphere of a snowy winter's day. This surprisingly colourful snow-covered landscape depicts the hamlet of Lavacourt, across the river from Vétheuil, where Monet had moved in 1878. It is a powerful combination of boldness and subtlety. Establishing a simple, triangular-based composition, and using thickly applied, *impasto* paint, Monet has created a delicate essay in pastel colours. The snow closest to where he placed his easel is painted in various shades of blue. For the cold waters of the Seine, against which the dark shape of the rowing boat is set, he has used an icy, absinthe green, contrasting with strokes of pinkish white. On the distant hillsides beyond, the pink gains precedence, with blue streaks indicating shadowy contours and creating a visual link between background and foreground.

PLATE 17
Claude Monet
The Custom Officer's House at Varengville, 1882

Perched on the edge of a towering cliff, its orange roof standing out in contrast with the calm blue waters of the English Channel, the custom's officer's house stands in splendid, if apparently precarious, isolation on the Normandy coast. During the 1880s, Monet became attracted to the remote and dramatic aspects of Nature, and he made numerous painting 'campaigns' to this spectacular stretch of coastline. This particular spot, where the chalk cliffs have split to create a huge gorge, was one of his favourite sites. He painted it almost 20 times in 1882 alone. In order to gain this vantage point, where the house and the undulating contours of the cliff edge are silhouetted against the sea, the artist had to make a laborious climb, and position himself on a grassy bluff across the gorge from the custom's house.

PLATE 18
Gustave Caillebotte
The Bridge over the Seine at Argenteuil, 1885

An immensely wealthy man, who often bought his friends' works, Gustave Caillebotte has mostly been remembered as a great collector rather than a great artist: the Impressionist paintings that he left to France form the core of the magnificent Musée d'Orsay collection. But he was also a gifted and original painter. This striking riverscape was painted near his home at Petit-Gennevilliers, across the river from Argenteuil. It is characteristic of his work in many ways: in its dramatic viewpoint, in the way architectural elements create a strong sense of geometry in the composition, and in the deliberate play between surface pattern and pictorial depth. Framed beneath the arch of the road bridge that crosses the Seine at Argenteuil – just a short distance away from the railway bridge in Monet's picture (*see* Plate 7) – a tug-boat chugs along the shimmering Seine. A tiny figure is silhouetted against the iron grid at road level, while below the bridge a wide band of mauve-blue shadow cuts across the green water.

PLATE 19

Berthe Morisot

Forest of Compiègne, 1885

Morisot's extraordinarily free, sketchy technique is well illustrated in this unusual landscape. In 1874, more than ten years before she painted it, her broadly handled paintings had so shocked her ex-teacher Joseph Guichard that he wrote to her mother, suggesting that the errant young lady should 'go to the Louvre twice a week,' stand before the Old Masters, and 'ask forgiveness for having attempted to say in oil what can only be said in watercolour.' Her painting had become increasingly loose and confident since then. In this airy, forest scene, much of the bare canvas remains visible, scarcely covered by the animated slashes of red, orange, white, blue and green. And there is a strong decorative quality in the way the slim, silvery tree trunks are set against rapidly scrubbed areas of green that indicate dense areas of undergrowth.

PLATE 20
Georges Seurat
Le Bec du Hoc, Grandcamp, 1885

Though very similar in unusual viewpoint and subject matter to Monet's *The Custom Officer's House at Varengville* (*see* Plate 17) this serene, stylized painting could not be more different in effect. Seurat began his works with open-air studies, but finished canvases such as this were the product of laborious work in the studio, when the artist systematically covered the canvas with regularly sized dots of pure colour, which were designed to gain vibrancy by partially merging in the viewer's eye. With this 'divisionist' technique, Seurat took the Impressionists' concern with colour perception to such an extreme that he completely went against the essential nature of Impressionist landscapes. The critic Félix Fénéon wrote, 'Seurat's seascapes give off calm and melancholy. They ripple monotonously as far as the distant point where the sky comes down.'

PLATE 21

Paul Cézanne

Mont Sainte-Victoire from the Large Pine Tree, 1885–7

Cézanne was 'passionately fond of the contours' of Provence, and was particularly drawn to this huge, rugged mountain that dominated the landscape near his home in Aix. He painted it some 60 times. This is one of several versions in which the mountain is seen framed by tall pine trees; its angular contours echoed by the branches. Cézanne worked painstakingly slowly as he painted his motif over and over again, analysing the structures and spatial relationships he saw in front of him – not trying to imitate them, but attempting to create their artistic equivalent in patches of colour applied with parallel strokes of the brush. Paintings such as this show a revolutionary approach to landscape painting, one that has its roots in Impressionism, but that looks forward to Cubism and abstract art.

PLATE 22
Paul Gauguin
Peasants and Haystacks, 1889

Gauguin came to art through Impressionism: he was a well-paid stockbroker when the experience of seeing the first Impressionist exhibition in 1874 made him decide to become a painter, and it was through painting out of doors with Pissarro and Cézanne that he began to develop his landscape style. But he grew disillusioned with Impressionism in the 1880s. This Brittany scene was painted when he was staying at an artists' colony in Pont-Aven, at a time when he was deliberately distancing himself from his old Impressionist colleagues. With its brightly coloured, simplified forms contained within sinuous, decorative contours, it is typical of his style at the time. 'I love Brittany,' he wrote. 'I find here the savage and the primitive. When my wooden clogs reverberate on this granite soil, I hear the muffled, heavy and powerful note that I seek in my painting.'

PLATE 23
Vincent van Gogh
Cornfield with Cypresses, 1889

'The cypresses occupy my thoughts constantly,' Vincent wrote to his brother Theo. 'They are as beautiful in line and proportion as Egyptian obelisks. And the green has a quality of such distinction. It is a splash of black in a sunny landscape.' Vincent painted this extraordinary landscape when he was in a mental asylum in Saint-Rémy in Provence. Tormented by hallucinations and suicidal feelings, he found some refuge in his art, and when he was well enough to leave the grounds, he would set up his easel in the nearby fields. Although his original dark style had changed drastically after contact with the Impressionists, landscapes such as this are clearly not aimed at rendering a visual impression of a scene: 'Instead of trying to depict exactly what is before my eyes, I am using colour... to express myself forcefully.' Here, the writhing rhythms create an unsettling emotional intensity, while the dark form of the cypress against the golden corn and blue sky may have been seen by the artist as a symbol of death.

PLATE 24
Claude Monet
Grainstacks at Sunset, Frosty Weather, 1891

'For me, a landscape … only exists by virtue of the air and light that surround it,' Monet once commented. In 1890, he began working on a series of paintings of the cone-shaped stacks that dotted the fields around his final home at Giverny, not focusing so much on the stacks themselves as on the quality of light around them. Changing his canvas as light effects and atmospheric conditions altered, he painted the stacks at different times of day, from late summer to deepest winter. He exhibited fifteen of the paintings together as a series, at a triumphant one-man show in 1891. In this glorious example, all detail melts away as the glowing sunset envelops the simplified form of the stack, and tinges the frost-covered ground with golds and pinks. The precise elements of the landscape – the stack, the distant trees, the houses – become almost 'unreadable' and the painting works as an abstract pattern of coloured paint.

PLATE 25
Alfred Sisley
Moret Bridge, 1893

Sisley was the only Impressionist to remain loyal to the principles of Impressionism throughout his life. He always maintained the practice of painting landscapes on the spot, attempting to capture the fleeting effects of Nature. River scenes recur in his work, as in that of the other Impressionists, but Sisley also had a particular preoccupation with bridges. Often, as here, they burst into the painting from the side, and lead the eye diagonally across a river to the far shore. In his later years, the artist repeatedly painted this particular bridge, which spanned the river Loing near his final home at Moret. Here, he has chosen to paint it on a clear, sun-drenched morning, with cotton-wool clouds dotting the bright blue sky. Regularly receding arches march across the river, their pale stone tinged with the multi-coloured reflections on the rippling water. The broadly handled, loose texture of the river's surface softens the rigorous geometry of the composition.